PATHS AND PUBS OF THE WYE VALLEY

Twelve circular walks leading off the Wye Valley Walk between
Hereford and Monmouth, each featuring a halfway pub.

Fully revised fourth edition by
Heather & Jon Hurley

Maps and drawings by David Grech BA, BArch, RIBA

Fineleaf Editions, 2008
www.fineleaf.co.uk

Fourth edition © 2008 Heather & Jon Hurley
ISBN 978 0 9557577 0 9

Design: Philip Gray
Text: Warnock Pro
Print: SS Media
Cover: Ross-on-Wye Across the River by David Grech
Forest Stewardship Council certified paper

Published by Fineleaf Editions 2008
Moss Cottage, Pontshill, Ross-on-Wye HR9 5TB
www.fineleaf.co.uk
fineleafbooks@mac.com

British Library Cataloguing in Publication Data
A catalogue record for this book is available from the British Library

CONTENTS

INTRODUCTION

By popular demand this walking guide of the Wye Valley has been revised for the fourth time. All of these interesting and varied circular routes which lead off the waymarked Wye Valley Walk, explore the unspoilt countryside between Hereford and the Welsh border town of Monmouth, and have been specially selected to feature a pub around the halfway point.

The Valley of the Wye is an Area of Outstanding Natural Beauty, where care is taken to conserve the countryside for the public's enjoyment. The tranquil Wye flows through this designated area on its way from the boggy mountains of Plynlimon in mid-Wales to join the Severn at Chepstow. The glorious Wye meanders on, chatteringly low at the height of summer, but dark and stormy, brimming with turgid flood water, in the rainy season. Farmers who live on its banks enjoy, as the Egyptians did when the Nile flooded, a precious inch or two of organic silt to help start their grass and crops growing with renewed energy the following spring.

On its way the great river, its belly full of fish, smoothly flows by the square grey pile above Mordiford where members of the Hereford family still live. Twisting back, mingling with its little sister the Lugg, it passes places with delightful Postman Pat names, like the three Greens; Sink, Fiddler's and Peartree. From here it sails past the modified remains of the once historic Aramstone, then on to Hoarwithy where the church of St. Catherine in all its odd but fascinating splendour peers down with its Tuscan tower. Llanfrother on the hill, where monks centuries ago plied their patient crafts, is next, then horseshoeing round to Sellack it slips under the bouncy suspension bridge below Caradoc, an Elizabethan mansion now undergoing renovation since being burnt down.

Next, past another attractive stretch at the quaintly named Hole-in-the Wall, before sailing between the legs of a shattered railway bridge at Backney, where pillars built with Victorian skill and formidable craftsmanship still defy the river's moods.

At Brampton Abbotts the upper tiers of Ross are now within sight and the river laps the restored ruins of Wilton Castle after making its much photographed curve under the eaves of Ross. Cubberley next, where a fine old house has been replaced by what may become a modern classic of architecture, and on to the more traditional, more easily accepted Hill Court, its majestic front turned away from the river. Rapidly now the Wye passes under the considerable shadow cast by the ample remains of Goodrich Castle, near to the ancient Flanesford Priory, now like many failing Wye Valley properties, bolstered by new money.

On to Courtfield, the ancient home of the Vaughan family, below Coldwell Rocks, wriggling around Symonds Yat to be gawked at by the throngs that occupy the rock every day of the year, especially now the Peregrine Falcons have become an annual floorshow. On the river flows, beside the newly accessible Coppet Hill, like its name, rusty in autumn with its bracken tinged with browns and ambers. Then far below the lofty Kymin where buckish young gentlemen disported themselves over two hundred years ago. Under the seventeenth century stone arched bridge at Monmouth, relentlessly flowing on to its meeting with the Severn at Chepstow. Truly a great river, and one that fishermen, farmers, canoeists and ramblers will hopefully bless for centuries to come.

The Wye Valley Walk, waymarked with a leaping salmon logo, is a long distance path of one hundred and fifty miles leading from Chepstow to Plynlimon. Throughout its length it closely follows the river, either beside its lush banks or above it following well-worn hilly paths through thick wooded slopes. The condition of the paths has improved (any footpath problems should be reported to the relevant authority) since the first edition, thanks to more regular usage, and maintenance by the County Councils.

The pubs too have improved, many of them Free Houses, owned, occupied and managed by families and are among the better ones. Since the previous edition only one pub has been replaced because of closure, although several have changed hands since we last visited, but most 'new brooms' are as good, if not better, than the originals. Menus have become more interesting, the accent being on home made, using fresh ingredients. Vegetarians, once pariahs, now have a section of most menus to themselves. Wine lists are getting longer and more adventurous too with a variety of local cider and beers on offer.

Pubs are more reflective places now, with less of the electric noises associated with the goggle-eyed bandits which greedily gobbled up small change while emitting ear piercing sounds. Children are catered for, and even under our licensing laws, provisions are made for youngsters who if with their parents, can sip a soft drink and eat a sandwich in a side room. Sitting outside is a real treat in summer, and most of the pubs in this book excel in this department. The Hope and Anchor steals the show with its beautiful riverside setting, but the Butcher's Arms, the Lough Pool, the Crown and the Green Man are not far behind. Live fires in winter are traditional and welcoming, and most of our inns provide this essential ingredient.

When soggy after a rain swept walk there is nothing more pleasant than steaming by a crackling log fire with a drink, a bowl of good home-made soup and a 'toastie'. Loos are important, and they score highly in our pubs. All twelve inns are different, some walkers will favour one more than another, a few are for the job in hand, while some would grace any pub guide in the country.

Walkers please note, these rambles may vary slightly according to season, and changes made by the land users. Lanes, tracks, footpaths, bridlepaths and byways are followed where the public have a right of way. It is advisable, however, to refer to the relevant Ordnance Survey Sheet, where all Rights of Way are clearly shown. Other items required on these walks are sensible footwear, lightweight waterproofs and a rucksack to carry a map, compass, first aid and money for refreshments.

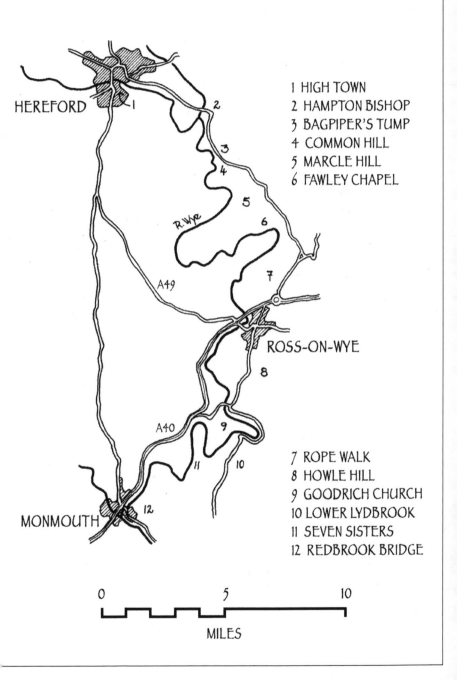

LOCATION OF WALKS

1 HIGH TOWN
2 HAMPTON BISHOP
3 BAGPIPER'S TUMP
4 COMMON HILL
5 MARCLE HILL
6 FAWLEY CHAPEL

7 ROPE WALK
8 HOWLE HILL
9 GOODRICH CHURCH
10 LOWER LYDBROOK
11 SEVEN SISTERS
12 REDBROOK BRIDGE

HEREFORD

R. Wye

A49

ROSS-ON-WYE

A40

MONMOUTH

0   5   10

MILES

Walk 1   **HIGH TOWN**

1½ miles around Hereford to the Spread Eagle
OS Explorer 189

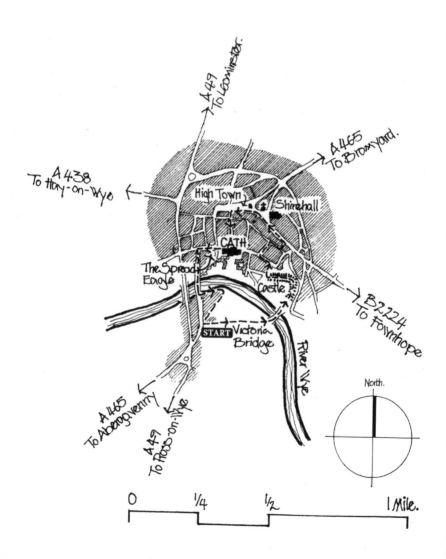

Hereford evolved over the centuries as a market town and cathedral city along the banks of the river Wye, which was crossed by an ancient ford before the building of the first bridge in the twelfth century. Our short stroll around the town will reveal some of Hereford's historic past, attractive features and pleasant views, with a pub pause at the Spread Eagle. A brief section of the Wye Valley Walk is followed for part of the way.

Route

The walk begins at the large car park beside the Hereford Leisure Pool (GR508394) where vehicles can be parked all day. For those without transport there are plenty of buses and trains to Hereford from the neighbouring towns. Take the path starting from the north-east corner of the car park. Walk across Bishop's Meadow where the path follows Row Ditch, a medieval earthwork. After enjoying the views of Dinedor and Aconbury Hills, the Wye Valley Walk is followed across the river Wye by the Victoria Suspension Bridge erected in 1898. After the crossing you leave the waymarked route which passes a former 18th century hospital. Our way, however, continues to the left and up some steps through pretty flower gardens leading to Castle Green.

Attractively laid out, the green is the site of an early Norman castle which suffered badly during the Civil War. The ramparts are followed to the right where at the highest point there are pleasant views of the surrounding countryside. Also to be seen on the far side of the remaining moat are the almshouses of St. Ethelbert, founded in 1225, and in the middle of the green a column in memory of Lord Nelson erected in 1809.

At the end of the ramparts turn right along a back lane, passing a striking house called the Fosse. Here a left turn leads into the attractive Castle Street. Before the Cathedral Close, turn right along Ferrers Street leading to East Street. Turn right, then left through the narrow Barroll Street, towards the centre of the town at St. Owens's Street, which is followed to the left. Walk past the Town Hall which was built in 1904, nearly opposite the Shire Hall designed by Robert Smirke, the architect of the British Museum. Now enter St. Peter's Square, where the church dates back to the late thirteenth century. Keep ahead for High Town, the original market place, and now a pleasant and traffic-free centre.

The superb timber framed Old House, built in 1621, cannot be missed (now a museum and open to the public). It is the only surviving building of the ancient Butcher's Row. Another feature in High Town is the Butter Market which may be entered by the door below the clock tower. Before you are tempted by the array of market stalls, remember the route soon leaves the bustling High Town to follow the signed passageway on the left to the Cathedral. The quiet Church Street boasts a varied collection of book, food, craft and map shops and leads into Cathedral Close. The Cathedral dating from 1080 is by far the most important building in the City for its history and architecture. Guide books are available in the Cathedral Gift Shop. Having explored the interior, leave the Close by the entrance opposite the imposing City Library and Museum, and bear left to meet King Street, where a refreshment break can be enjoyed at the Spread Eagle.

The Spread Eagle   (Tel: 01432 272205)
The Spread Eagle, once an old coaching inn, is now a busy pub, efficiently managed by three women. Situated practically next door to the magnificent Cathedral, it offers visitors and locals an international menu and plenty of space to enjoy it.

Hereford Cathedral & the old Wye Bridge

Pictures of Olde Hereforde adorn the walls and in the painted stone fireplace a gas fire burbles in winter. The bar is oak panelled and the Jacobean staircase is one of the few reminders of a bygone age, fruit machines, a juke box and piped hits of yesteryear remind us things do change.

The menu is exotic in its spread, everything from New Zealand Mussels, Mongolian Fire Pot, Jerk Jamaica Sword Fish, and Tex Mex. To the homely 'My Mum's Tangy Cheese Potato Pie' and judging by the number of different flavoured Sausages, eleven in all, one can't help thinking the Chef has a thing about the humble banger.

There are Sandwiches, Salads, Baguettes, and Steaks galore. And heaps of tempting Deserts, served with locally made Ice Cream. Our favourite was Caramelised Whisky and Bread and

Butter Pudding. The oft neglected veggie will have a field day at The Spread. Children too are fussed over.

The list of beers on tap is a who's who of popular, lightweight brews, but a serious Real Ale or two is also available, along with Guinness chilled or chambre'd. The wine list is tiny but it comes in Red, White, Pink and Fizzy, served by bottle or glass. Upstairs there is a spacious room to take the overspill.

Return

After lunch continue along King Street to the crossroads, take a left turn down Bridge Street to the fifteenth century Wye Bridge, built of stone with parapets and six arches. It is worth lingering a while to admire the river, the new Greyfriars Bridge, built in the 1960s, and the popular view of the Cathedral. Beyond is the Bishop's Palace, which dates from the twelfth century. Having crossed the Wye, immediately turn left along the riverbank once the site of Cathedral Wharf. Now signed as the Wye Valley Walk it passes Old Ford House, its name a reminder of an earlier river crossing before the bridge was built. The path leads alongside Bishop's Meadow, but turn right here across the meadow to the car park next to the Leisure Pool.

Walk 2 HAMPTON BISHOP

3½ mile walk from Mordiford Church to the Bunch of Carrots
OS Explorer 189

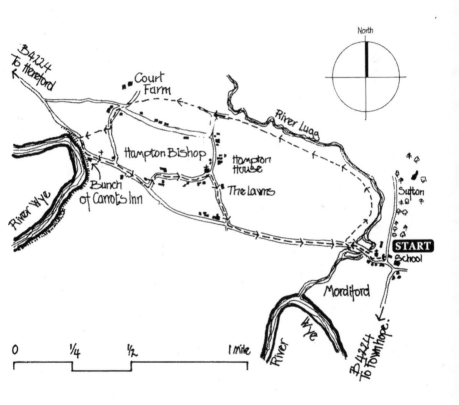

This is a leisurely stroll suitable for all ages, and can be equally enjoyed in mid-summer or in the depths of winter. Mordiford is a compact village with a church, old rectory, inn, shop and cottages neatly set between the hills of Haugh Wood and the banks of the

River Lugg, a tributary of the nearby Wye. From the church at Mordiford the Wye Valley Walk is followed along the flood banks of the Lugg to the attractive village of Hampton Bishop, where the comforts of the inn can be sampled before returning.

Route

This gentle walk starts from the church at Mordiford (GR 571375) where parking is available. Opposite the church observe the Victorian school, opened in 1873, and still in use. Walk through the Iych gate under the overhanging branches of an old yew tree, to the church dedicated to the Holy Rood. The Norman doorway remains, but the tower was rebuilt in 1811 replacing a central tower on which a twelve foot green dragon with a red mouth and tongue was painted in the fourteenth century to illustrate a local legend.

Leave the graveyard by the smaller gate, pass the entrance to the old rectory, now converted into several dwellings, and cross the River Lugg by a fine arch bridge dating back to the fourteenth century. Here the Wye Valley Walk is joined and the leaping salmon waymarks indicate the way. From Mordiford Bridge pleasant views can be seen of the village, the wooded hills, and Sufton, a large eighteenth century house. The waymarks lead to the right along the flood bank of the Lugg to the end of this large field where, to the right, buildings of Sufton and Old Sufton with its walled garden and dovecote will be seen. Ahead, are the church and houses of Hampton Bishop, surrounded by lovely countryside, marred only by pylons in this particular spot.

The Wye Valley Walk leaves the willow lined Lugg and turns left into the village to meet Rectory Road, but our way continues ahead through fields and gates, and over stiles until reaching a farm track at Court Farm. Here turn left then right to rejoin

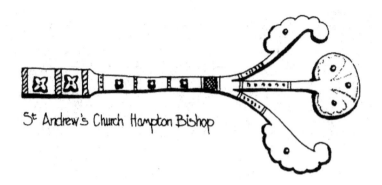

St Andrew's Church Hampton Bishop

the Wye Valley Walk passing thatched black and white cottages and several modern houses. In winter the naked trees in the orchards and gardens provide useful sustenance for hungry blackbirds and fieldfares. Continue along a narrow footpath on the right, over a stile, and through a level paddock where a further stile leads to the Hereford to Fownhope Road. Cross the road carefully, to reach the Bunch of Carrots Inn.

The Bunch of Carrots Inn (Tel: 01432 870237)
The Carrots gets its unusual name, according to local legend, from an exclusive salmon pool in the nearby Wye. It has been an inn for at least one and a half centuries and was fairly recently considerably altered with multiple rooms and cosy snugs. It is comfortable, warm and well furnished with the walls covered in a most eclectic selection of pictures, everything from military scenes and bird prints to amusing fishing sketches. Oak beams abound and there is a fire, a most welcoming sight for the freezing rambler, with plenty of room for stretching tired legs.

The menu ranges from Children's Portions to Baguettes, Soups, and Salads, Pan Fried Chicken Livers, Venison Steaks, Cornish Whole Lemon Sole, to Homemade Creamy Brie and Mushroom Risotto, all served with appropriate vegetables.

There is also a splendid carvery as well as 'dishes of the day' and a nice line in puds. The 'Casque Marque' approved beers include Courage's Best, with The Wye Valley and Spinning Dog breweries supplying locally brewed ales. Wine can be purchased by glass or bottle.

The Carrots is an interesting, comfortable and relaxing place for walkers, drivers or anyone else for that matter. Children are welcome and there is ample parking. The service is swift and friendly and no extraneous sounds disturb the peace.

Return

A longer alternative return, avoiding a stretch along the road, is now available. Follow the signed and waymarked footpath from the pub for three and a half miles leading around a meander of the Wye to join the Lugg before reaching Mordiford Bridge.

Otherwise leave the inn by turning right along the road towards Mordiford. After passing the former Methodist Chapel, take the second turning on the left, called Whitehall Road, which winds around pretty thatched cottages before reaching Hampton Bishop Church. Well kept, the church, dedicated to St. Andrew, has an unusual timbered tower and is worth a visit to see Norman remains, a Jacobean pulpit and interesting monuments. From the church gate cross the road and follow the right hand fork leading in front of The Lawns, a Georgian brick built house with its outbuildings converted into cottages. Soon the Hereford to Fownhope Road is met, where a left turn is taken. A short stretch along this busy route will lead back across the Lugg to Mordiford Church.

Walk 3 BAGPIPER'S TUMP

5 mile walk from Fownhope to the Moon Inn, Mordiford
OS Explorer 189

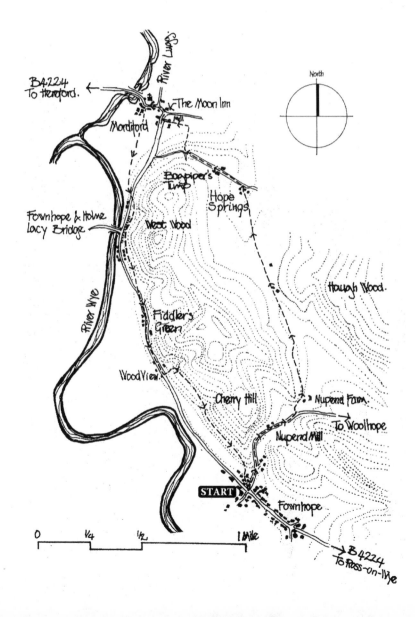

This picturesque ramble takes in some prettily named places: Hope Springs, Bagpiper's Tump, Fiddler's Green and Cherry Hill. The section along the Wye Valley Walk leads through a delightful valley before reaching the Moon Inn at Mordiford. The return route along wooded hillsides offers outstanding views of the Wye.

Route

The walk begins from the minor crossroads at Fownhope (GR 572346) where cars can be parked in the village. From the crossroads follow the Woolhope Road and notice on the right hand comer a drinking fountain, erected in 1897 to commemorate Queen Victoria's Diamond Jubilee The road shortly passes the disused mill at Nupend, and a little further on, the Wye Valley Walk is joined. Turn left and follow the waymarked path through the gates and above Nupend Farm, where the track leads into wide fields through a broad open valley with the wooded hill of Haugh Wood on the right and mixed woodland of Cherry Hill, Fownhope Park and West Wood to the west.

A couple of isolated cottages are passed before reaching a farm track leading to the farm and converted barns at Hope Springs. The waymarks clearly direct a turn to the left, along a lane passing pretty cottages at Bagpiper's Tump. Bear right and down to a stile into a neat orchard where the tower of Mordiford Church comes into view. A further stile leads out of the orchard into the yard of a tall old mill, which still boasts the rusting remains of its water wheel. On reaching the road turn right, where the Moon Inn will be seen ahead.

The Moon Inn   (Tel: 01432 870236)

The Moon is a fifteenth century stone and timber built local in the centre of the village of Mordiford. It boasts two neat bars, one with quoits and darts, and the other with a roaring log fire in winter. There is also a separate dining room and a pleasant garden for sitting out in on sunny days. It enjoys good views of the surrounding hills.

Walkers are made welcome by a friendly staff. The beers include Well's Bombardier, the Wye Valley Brewery's Butty Bach and Carling's Black Label. Local Cider and pure Fruit Juices are also available.

Bar Snacks abound and there is comprehensive range of reasonably priced dishes on menus and blackboards, including a selection of Fish dishes, Home Made Curries, Lasagna, Lamb and Apricot Pie, Faggots with Gravy and an intriguing number of Steaks with names like Blue Moon, Washington and Mexican. Children and Vegetarians are catered for and there are Gluten Free Sausages. Portions are generous and the wine list is cheap and acceptable with a very inexpensive and light House Wine Selection. Traditional roasts are served on Sundays.

Return

From the Moon Inn follow the Hereford road to view Mordiford's thirteenth century church, fourteenth century bridge and Georgian rectory before returning. Beside the village shop follow the Wye Valley Walk for a few yards until reaching a stile on the left. Follow the field path ahead over stiles and upon reaching the road turn right. Opposite the next cottage, climb a signed but sometimes overgrown footpath to a forest track, where a right turn is taken. Here one catches glimpses of the Wye, twisting and turning in the valley below, spanned by the modern Fownhope and Holme Lacy Bridge constructed in 1973, replacing a former iron structure. The forest track continues until descending to the road just before Fiddler's Green. Follow the road to the left past a few largish houses, including Morney Cross, Wood View and Rock House. Beyond the latter a signed footpath on the left leads up through a field alongside the boundary of the terraced gardens of Rock House.

At the corner of the field, go through the deer gate and turn immediately right. From here the path is more clearly defined, skirting the wooded hills with a fence on the right hand side. In springtime violets, primroses, bluebells and wood anemones are seen in abundance in these woods, again the views of the Wye are quite outstanding. On reaching new houses at Fownhope, continue behind gardens and within 200 yards turn right over a stile into a small housing estate. Follow the road to the main Fownhope Road, where a left turn brings you back to the crossroads.

The Drinking Fountain, Fownhope, erected in 1897

Walk 4 **COMMON HILL**

3½ miles around Fownhope to the Green Man Inn
OS Explorer Sheet 189

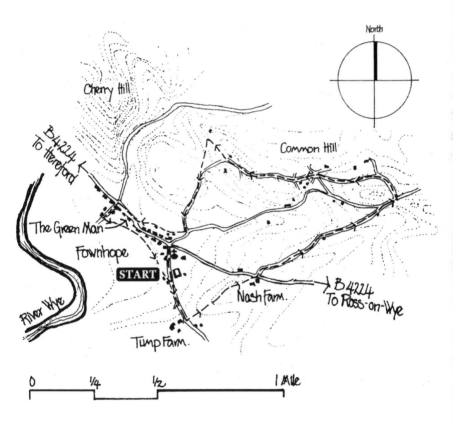

Fownhope lies between the meandering Wye and the irregular wooded slopes of Common Hill. The expanding village has a thriving community, centred along the route of the old Hereford to Gloucester Road, where shops, inns, a school and a beautiful Norman church are conveniently situated. This ramble follows paths and lanes leading to Common Hill where the Wye Valley Walk is joined. Extensive views may be appreciated from the hill before descending to the Green Man Inn at Fownhope.

Route

The walk starts from the entrance to the sports pavilion (GR579342) where cars may be parked. Before following Capler Lane away from the village, St. Mary's Church is worth a visit, with its well-preserved Norman tympanum, amongst other historical items on display in this spacious building with its fourteenth century tower and spire.

Follow the lane towards Capler, passing some interesting houses of varied architectural styles. At the top of the hill, opposite Tump Farm situated in a prominent position, turn sharp left up the steep steps, over a stile and into fields. Suddenly there are fine views of Fownhope, Haugh Woods, Holme Lacy, Capler Hill and the Valley of the Wye. Keep ahead until reaching the leaning stone wall surrounding Nash Farm. Bear left here over a stile, then turn right, passing the almost derelict Georgian farmhouse, before joining the road at a gate.

Cross the Fownhope to Ross Road (B4224) and follow the quiet Hawker's Lane ahead, leading up to Common Hill. In springtime the banks between the pretty cottages are covered with snowdrops, violets, primroses and daffodils. The views are ever changing as you climb to over 500 feet. Just beyond an attractive white washed cottage the waymarks of the Wye Valley Walk are followed to the left, along the cottage drive, then slightly right to follow a sunken green lane, probably used for transporting lime from the numerous lime pits on Common Hill. The waymarked path crosses an open area called Monument Hill, now a nature reserve, where the limestone grassland attracts many gaily-coloured butterflies during summer. A further stile is crossed, and here a well-defined track leads to a clearing where a network of paths and lanes meet. Continue following the Wye Valley Walk across the ridge of Common Hill.

Before descending, a black and white cottage is passed on the right. This is where one leaves the Wye Valley Walk to follow a track on the left, going downhill through the trees, then across a field, where a further track is joined leading down to the outskirts of Fownhope. At a new housing estate go right along Church Croft, and follow the paved path between bungalows to Court Orchard. Beside the village school and its large sign follow the footpath on the left leading back to the B4224, where the Green Man will be seen on the right.

The Norman Tympanum in Fownhope Church.

The Green Man   (Tel: 01432 860243)

The spacious Green Man, after a series of managers, is now a Millfields Inn. Said to date from the fifteenth century, it retains some old style charm and boasts a pleasant garden for dining al fresco. There are several bars, the main one is spacious, oak beamed, with boxing prints and a fire to toast the toes of the winter walker.

The menu is extensive, with a welcome nod towards green issues, featuring 'Breast of Free Association' chicken, 'Outdoor Reared' pork chops, sensitively sourced steaks, 'Flake Seared' Scottish Salmon and breast of tenderly raised Duck, and Fresh Fish delivered daily. There is also that almost forgotten 60s classic, good old New Zealand Lamb, as well as substantial burgers made from tender beef. There are Snacks galore, several of them homemade, thick Homemade Soups with Garlic Bread, a Sweets, and popular Sunday Roasts. Veggies and Children are welcome.

The beer is well kept with Adnams Broadside and others guesting, and Bombardier and John Smith on tap. Guinness, Boddington and Carling Black Label are always available, as are lagers and local ciders. The wine list is adventurous by pub standards. Service was efficient and the atmosphere friendly. Customers included the tweeds and Telegraph variety, youngsters and the rustic chat club; a good pub attracts all sorts. There are banqueting facilities, accommodation, a playground, and ample parking.

An item of interest to fans of pugilism is that the legendary Tom Spring, Bare-knuckle Champion of all England, in 1823/4 was born a few doors down from the pub. Rumour has it he did a stint as landlord. He didn't, but it's a good story! Fight fans might like to take a look at the mural in the dining room, featuring a potted history of the pub, including Tom Spring's alleged part in it.

Return

After refreshments, continue along the road towards Hereford to a minor crossroads. Take the left turning to Ferry Lane, which as the name suggests leads to the River Wye. Up to the 1920's a boat carried travellers across the river to Holme Lacy. Opposite the former Forge and Ferry Inn follow a signed path, cross a brook and continue to the left, around the side of a large field. Walk behind inns and houses where glimpses of the Wye may be seen. Another brook and stile is crossed leading onto a football pitch. At the next cottage turn right to return to the sports pavilion.

Walk 5 **MARCLE HILL**

12 mile walk from Brockhampton to the
Butcher's Arms, Woolhope
OS Explorer Sheet 189

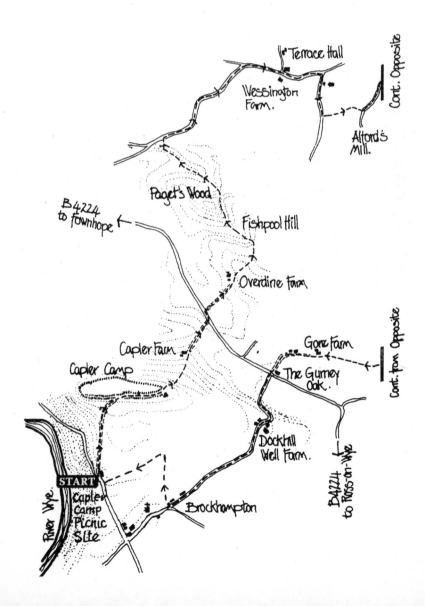

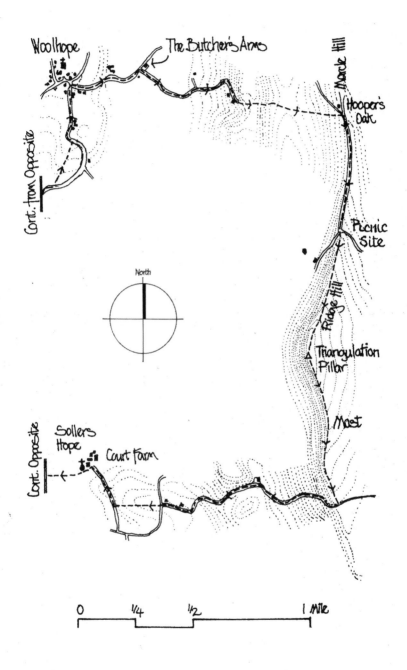

Woolhope

The Butcher's Arms

Marcle Hill

Hooper's Oak

Cont. from Opposite

North

Picnic Site

Ridge Hill

Triangulation Pillar

Mast

Sollers Hope

Cont. Opposite

Court Farm

0   1/4   1/2   1 Mile

This superb walk combines everything, from an Iron Age hillfort at Capler, an eighteenth century lime kiln at Woolhope, to the towering modern TV mast on Ridge Hill. Quiet lanes, pleasant paths, and the Wye Valley Walk, lead from the scenic picnic site at Capler across rolling hills to Woolhope, before returning along the ridge from Much Marcle to Sollers Hope. Spectacular views of the Malvern Hills and the Black Mountains may be enjoyed and admired throughout this longer walk, and it is worth the effort to visit The Butcher's Arms at Woolhope.

Route

Parking is available at Capler Picnic Site, (GR 591323) but before heading north along the Wye Valley Walk, glance at one of our favourite views of the River Wye. Cross the road to follow the waymarked path along a track, then diagonally across a conifer plantation, and turn right when reaching the double ramparts of Capler Camp, an Iron Age fort standing at 600 feet, with magnificent views.

An isolated cottage and barn at Capler are passed before bearing sharp left down a flight of wooden steps. The way continues ahead through fields and over stiles then left to arrive at the lane serving Caplor Farm. A right turn leads to the main Ross to Fownhope Road (B4224), which is followed to the left for a few yards. Another right turn to Overdine Farm is clearly indicated, where the waymarked path leads through fields around the farm, up Fishpool Hill to Paget's Wood and needs to be carefully followed.

Paget's Wood is sixteen acres of mixed woodland owned by the Herefordshire Nature Trust. The walk through the nature reserve is quite delightful, with a great variety of wild flowers and small birds in abundance. The limestone of the Woolhope Dome has now been reached, and the first disused lime kilns will be seen in this wood, almost hidden by debris. A lovely open valley leads across to a tarmaced lane, which is followed to the right leaving the route of the Wye Valley Walk.

After about half a mile of bends and hills, keep right at the next junction to pass the attractive black and white buildings of Terrace Hall standing opposite Wessington Farm. Take the next right hand lane and within 500 yards follow a bridleway on the left through a field gate. It leads parallel along the banks of a brook meeting a lane leading to Alford's Mill. Turn left along the lane and beyond a right hand bend, turn left over a stile, where a field path leads ahead over a footbridge and across meadows to join a tarmac lane. Bear left towards Woolhope, which is soon reached.

Woolhope lies in an elevated position, and contains a pleasing mixture of stone and brick buildings clustered around a church dedicated to St. George and dating from the early thirteenth century. Standing next to the church is the popular Crown Inn but if you do not wish to explore the village, turn right immediately at the village along the tarmac lane leading to the Butcher's Arms, lying a little distance from the village in a most delightful setting.

The Butcher's Arms (Tel: 01432 860281)

This pleasant and deservedly popular inn compliments an excellent walk. Set amid attractive farmland with a stream trickling through the small garden; with its low beam ceilings (mind your head!), cosy atmosphere and log fires in winter, an absolute essential for the sodden walker, it is the ideal place to slip away from the bustle of modern living. Old bar furniture and a profusion of monochrome prints, featuring various rustic pursuits, help create the right ambience.

The co-owner being a chef means the menu is satisfying and imaginative. Starters include Pan Fried Black Pudding with a tasty salad. Prime Herefordshire Beef, Pork Valentine, Faggots, Breaded Turkey Escalope, and BBQ Spare Ribs and Poached Salmon are among the mains. Vegetarians have a good selection to choose from, including Home Made Quiche and Pasta Arrabiata. The Children's Menu list several popular items. Salads, Sandwiches and Soups offered at reasonable prices.

The beers include products from the reliable Wye Valley and Hook Norton breweries. An ever changing stream of quality 'Guest Brews' keep the CAMRA supporters happy. A pleasant bottle of Red, White, or Pink can be found among the wines on offer. Having Mateus Rose as the House Pink is a nice retro touch.

Happily no sounds other than the whistling of birds in the fields outside intrude to spoil the harmonious atmosphere, and a separate room caters for the darts chucking community.

Lime Kilns on the approach to Marcle Hill

Outside jaded walkers may sit in the shade and take their well-earned repast in idyllic comfort, before setting off for the second, and equally searching, part of this very fine walk.

Return

Drag yourself away from the inn by following the narrow lane alongside the car park, crossing the brook that runs through the pub's garden. This old lane steeply ascends the wooded hill and turns sharply right before passing an isolated dwelling, after which a gate leads onto open hillside where further lime kilns can be investigated. At over 500 feet panoramic views of the Herefordshire countryside and the Black Mountains may be savoured. The well defined track leads down the left hand side of a small wood. The path then continues in a straight line through fields, descending, then climbing to the roadside opposite Hooper's Oak at the southern end of Marcle Hill, where the Herefordshire Trail is joined.

A right turn along the road is the start of the scenic ridge walk, overlooking Ledbury and the Malvern Hills from a height of over 800 feet. At the next road junction beside a picnic site keep straight ahead up stone and earth steps, cross the stile and continue along Ridge Hill.

The path leads over stiles, through fields, then along an enclosed path, past the triangular pillar and the TV mast supported by huge cables. A little further on the path descends to a wooden stile in the corner of a field where it meets a sunken track. Here leave the Herefordshire Trail and turn right along the track, gradually descending through woodland and past several buildings, and more disused lime kilns on the right. At the top of the kiln a large pit lies above the furnace holes, where fired lime was produced from layers of coal and limestone. Before crossing a brook the track becomes tarmaced, winding its way down to meet a lane at Sollers Hope.

Cross the lane and enter the field opposite over a stile, and follow an undefined path straight across the field to Church Lane. Turn right towards the secluded church standing next to Court Farm, an attractive sixteenth century black and white building. Keep left of the fourteenth century church at Sollers Hope and continue through the graveyard to a gate where a waymarked path leads from the footbridge straight across a field. At the next stile continue ahead keeping to the left hand side through two fields. At the left hand corner turn sharp left over a stile and proceed in the same direction around Gore Farm. Within a few hundred yards a stile on the right leads into an unmade lane leading past cottages to reach the main road beside the former Gurney Oak Inn.

Cross the road, follow the narrow winding lane up past Dockhill Well Farm, and within a mile turn right at the telephone box, or keep ahead to visit Brockhampton Church built in 1902 epitomising the spirit of the Arts and Crafts movement. From the telephone box the path leads along a track to a cottage. Bear diagonally right through the field to a stile, and continue in the same direction to the next stile. Here turn sharp left along the field boundary to return to the picnic site at Capler Camp.

The View West from Ridge Hill, Towards Capler Camp & The Black Mountains

Walk 6 FAWLEY CHAPEL

10 mile walk from Hole-in-the-Wall to the
Lough Pool Inn, Sellack
OS Explorer Sheet 189

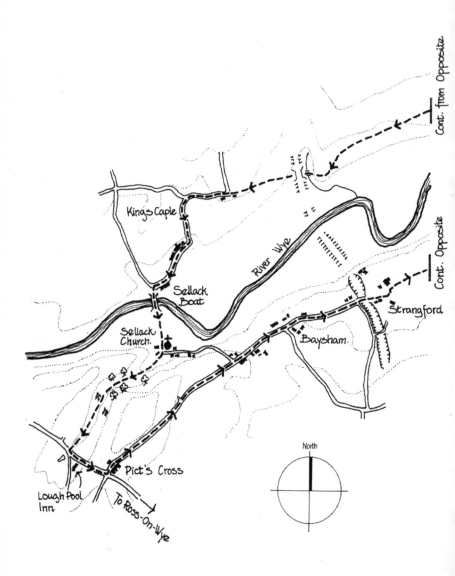

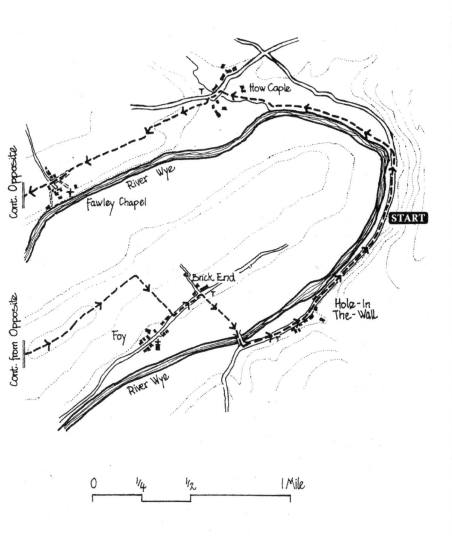

From a delightful stretch of the River Wye at Hole-in-the-Wall, footpaths and bridleways lead through the heart of the scenic Wye Valley to Sellack. Here the river is crossed by a swaying suspension bridge, then a delightful footpath is followed to the Lough Pool Inn. The return continues along lanes and paths offering splendid views in all directions of the Wye.

Route

From the limited parking beside the Perrystone Estate sign at Hole-in-the- Wall (GR 617295) proceed in a northerly direction following the waymarks of the Wye Valley Walk to the banks of the Wye, where the riverside path eventually veers right alongside a brook to join the road at How Caple. From here to Kings Caple the route follows the line of an old Roman Road instead of the Wye Valley Walk. Turn left at the telephone box and through a gate across the field towards a house. Bear right keeping the field boundaries on the left until reaching a stile, where the way continues in the same direction on the other side of the hedge. On approaching buildings, follow a short track between houses to meet a tarmac lane at Fawley Chapel.

The Norman Chapel, neatly tucked away, can be viewed on the left; but our way continues ahead along a little used bridleway, through a series of gates across a yard. Keep to the right hand side of the fields until reaching a gate ahead, from here the line of the bridleway goes straight across a large field towards a gate beside an oak. Cross the gate, keep close to the right hand hedge, pass the scanty remains of Mutloe's Barn then descend and bear slightly right through a narrow gate. Cross a marshy brook by a concrete bridge beside a pool, then proceed ahead under a disused railway bridge. Now ascend through fields to Ingsbury Cottage at Kings Caple.

Follow the tarmac lane ahead, fork left at the junction and descend to cottages at Sellack Boat. At a sharp bend, turn left along a signed path leading to a suspension bridge spanning the Wye. This late nineteenth century construction replaced a former ferry. At the other side, walk across the riverside meadows following a well used path to Sellack Church. This is the only English church dedicated to the Celtic St. Tysilio who lived during the seventh century. The building has an unusual layout and contains many interesting monuments.

From the church turn left along a tarmac lane and within a few yards turn right across a stile to follow a signed footpath along the banks of a brook. At the end of the meadow cross another stile, bear slightly right , then ahead through woodland lying above a group of fishponds from which the brook flows. Cross a stile out of the woods and continue up a delightful valley to reach a stile leading to an enclosed path and stile opposite the Lough Pool Inn.

The Lough Pool Inn   (Tel: 01989 730236)

It is always a treat halfway round a leisurely walk to see this little black and white Free House with its rustic seats and old cider press. The present owners have been in charge for a few

The Lough Pool Inn

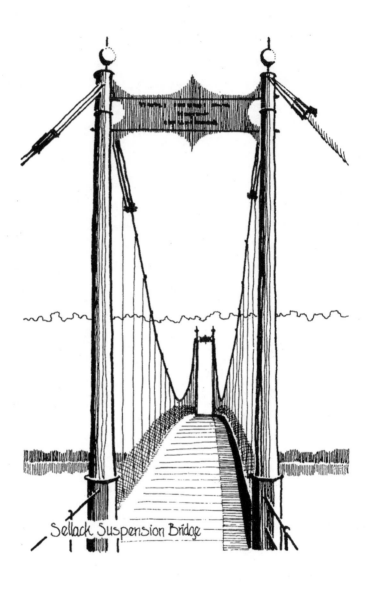

Sellack Suspension Bridge

years and a packed car park bears witness to the fine job they are doing in keeping both visitor and local fed and watered. Apart from the friendly welcome, and in winter the sweet smelling fire, the Lough Pool, now sporting a Michelin Bib Gourmand gong, is spick and span with its stone flagged floors; old polished furniture and exposed beams. There is but one bar these days with a couple of nooks and adjoining dining room with accommodation for upwards of fifty diners.

The menu is full of eye-catching grub, vegetarian and otherwise, much of it locally sourced. Fish, meat and cheese dishes are attractively served with salads, vegetables in season, or proper, hand sliced, chips. Specialities include Slow Cooked Blade of locally bred and reared Beef, Weobley Pork, Pot Roasted Organic Chicken, and fish from a Welsh Smokery. The Cheese Board includes local cheeses including the strong smelling but delicious Stinking Bishop.

The beer is always in good condition and as well as Guest Brews, includes Wye Valley Butty Bach and John Smith. Broome Farm Ciders, made from traditional cider apples, is brewed just down the road. The wine list is varied with several dozen from which to choose.

Electrical gadgets are neither seen nor heard, and there is not even a dart board. Walkers and children are welcome, though the former might be asked to park their muddy footwear outside, a small price to pay to enjoy one of the consistently finest pubs in Herefordshire.

Return
From the inn follow the road towards Ross, but at the top of the hill turn left at Pict's Cross along a pleasant tarmac lane for about one mile leading to Baysham and Strangford. Where the lane turns sharply right keep ahead along a lane crossing over the remains of the Hereford, Ross, Gloucester Railway line, where a deep cutting has been used as a landfill tip, now

reinstated as a meadow. The stone walls of a former bridge are the only remainders of this railway. Pass some cottages before reaching a farmyard, here keep left of a pool and proceed along a track following a waymarked path one side arid then another of the field boundary until reaching a swing-gate.

From this point the path is undefined but continue in the same direction until reaching a swing-gate on the right. Scramble between the hedge and a tiny reservoir and descend a sloping field. Keep on the right and walk around a farmyard before meeting the road at Foy.

Turn left along the road and opposite cottages at Brick End turn right following a signed and clearly defined footpath leading between fields to Foy suspension bridge. Linger awhile on this bridge to savour this wonderful stretch of the Wye where canoeists, fishermen, bird watchers and walkers enjoy an unspoilt and peaceful scene. A bridle bridge was first erected here in 1876, but was washed away by floods and replaced in 1921. Having crossed the Wye turn left along a tarmac lane leading back past farms and cottages to Hole-in-the- Wall. After crossing a cattle grid return to the start within half a mile.

Walk 7   ROPE WALK

7½ mile walk from Hole-in-the-Wall to the Hope and Anchor Inn, Ross-on-Wye
OS Explorer Sheet 189

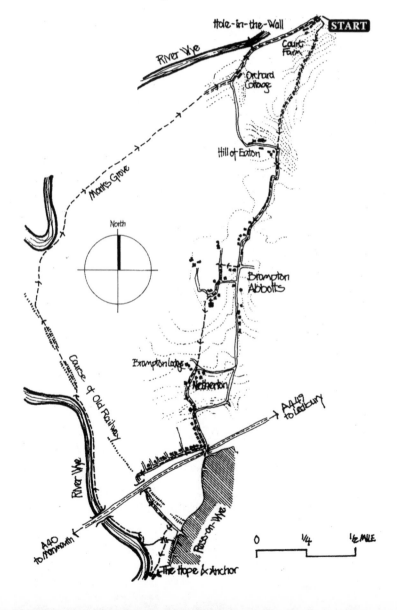

Hole-in-the-Wall refers to a collection of attractive cottages situated in Foy, a beautiful riverside parish divided by the meandering River Wye. Walkers can park their cars here before setting off across hills, along winding lanes and through the quiet village of Brampton Abbotts before reaching the market town of Ross-on-Wye and the Hope and Anchor Inn. The return route along the Wye Valley Walk closely follows the banks of the river.

Route
Limited car parking is available at Hole-in-the-Wall (GR 611286). Follow the signed footpath 'Brampton Abbotts' which leads between a post box and Aberhall Cottages. Where the footpath enters the field, turn right and walk uphill to the next gate, which leads onto a sunken lane passing behind Court Farm, an Adventure Holiday Centre. This grassy track bears slightly to the left, leading steeply to another gate. At the top of this hill there are some splendid views of Foy with its old church and suspension bridge spanning the Wye. Now above an ancient L-shaped earthwork, the way continues ahead through fields, keeping to the left hand side until an enclosed path leads to an open field. Walk straight ahead where a steep climb leads to a stile beside a footpath sign, which can clearly be seen to the left of the farm buildings at Hill of Eaton.

Follow the tarmac lane to the left around the bends for about half a mile. On approaching Brampton Abbotts the wooded hills of Chase and Penyard beyond Ross become visible. At a road junction look out for an overgrown OS benchmark enclosed by iron railings, then turn right up steps: cross a stile and walk straight through the field towards a cottage, once the village smithy. Continue ahead following the signed footpath through

Cottages at Hole-in-the-Wall

the orchard where the next stile leads onto a narrow metalled lane. Here turn left and at the bend keep ahead along a signed footpath to reach St. Michael's Church, Brampton Abbotts. This neat building with its timber bell turret dates back to the Normans and has a pleasing fourteenth century porch. Proceed through the churchyard with its varied and interesting headstones and leave by the iron swing gate. A well-trodden path leads through fields, where the bustle of Ross-on-Wye can be heard.

Shortly the farm and barns at Netherton are reached, continue ahead to follow a lane with Brampton Lodge on your right. Another uphill climb leads to the Brampton Road, followed right to the outskirts of Ross. Before the modern road bridge turn right along Greytree Road, leading down, around and under another bridge to meet Homs Road, Walk through a car park on the right and cross the footbridge over the Rudhall Brook. Keep ahead along the wide path known as the Rope Walk through the riverside meadows to the Hope and Anchor Inn.

The Hope and Anchor Inn   (Tel: 01989 563003)

The Hope and Anchor, a Banks pub, is attractively situated on the famous Horseshoe Bend of the river Wye, below Ross-on-Wye. A former innkeeper kept a pleasure boat here for his clients' use, while another landlord regularly rowed downstream to collect withies near Wilton Castle for his spare time occupation as a basket weaver. The Boat bar actually contains two boats. One, the Gypsy Queen, is now used as the counter but in its heyday it transported holiday makers up and down this lovely stretch of river.

The rowing boat which now hangs a little ignominiously from the ceiling above the pool table, once bulged with freshly netted salmon. To complete the nautical theme a small anchor, fished from the river by a diver some years ago, is displayed in the bar. A selection of sepia snaps of Ross by the riverside adorns the walls. Upstairs the Parlour is a comfortable and quieter room with a Victorian flavour.

The three hundred years old Hope offers a selection of both draught and bottled beers. These include the brewer's range, Bank's Original, Old Empire, and Marston's Pedigree, plus Fosters, Harp and Strongbow Cider. Guest brews are offered and Local Ciders are planned The wine list is tiny but cheap.

The menu is extensive and competitively priced, ideal ramblers fare, with Soups, Salads, Sandwiches and Baguettes, as well as Dishes of the Day. Steaks, Roasts, Curries, Lasagnes,

Prawns and Smoked Haddock, with Chips or without are also offered. Among the Puds an eye catcher is the Homemade Bailey's Cheese Cake. Children, vegetarians, canoeists and fishermen are welcome. There is ample parking and even a place to tie up one's boat.

The Hope enjoys spacious grounds with attractive river views, and provides a pleasant spot all year round for visitors and locals alike. Bands play everything from Jazz to Blues in summer, and the Morris Men cavort occasionally when weather permits.

Return

Leave the inn and walk to the rive bank, turn right to follow the Wye Valley Walk back to Hole-in-the- Wall. After re-crossing the Rudhall Brook, go around the boat house and under the modern river bridge; the path continues along the riverside for nearly a mile. This is a popular haunt for fishermen, swans, herons and wild ducks. The route bears right and follows a stretch of the disused Hereford, Ross, Gloucester Railway track, which operated between 1855 and 1964. The remaining hedgerows provide a useful habitat for wildlife. The waymarked path leaves the railway track as indicated before reaching Backney, where an iron memorial cross on the river bank may be seen. The waymarks lead on alongside a replanted wood called Monks Grove and continues through level pastures and fertile fields.

Opposite Foy Church, which is situated on the far side of the Wye, the path leads up to a gate and stile, where a short track joins the road. Turn left passing the isolated Orchard Cottage, and observe on your left Foy Bridge built in 1921, replacing a former bridge washed away by heavy floods. Within a quarter of a mile the cottages at Hole-in-the-Wall will be reached.

Walk 8   Howle Hill

5½ mile walk from Hom Green, Ross-on-Wye
to the Mill Race, Walford
OS Explorer Sheet 189

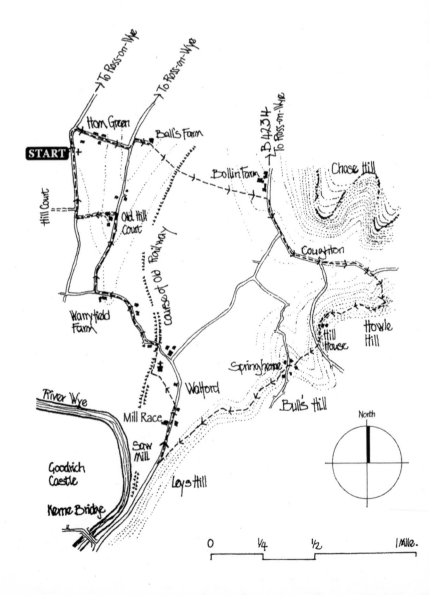

This walk follows a superb section of the Wye Valley Walk across the steep slopes of Howle, Bull's and Ley's Hills lying to the south of Ross-on-Wye. A gentler stretch is first followed through low-lying meadows from the quiet hamlet of Hom Green before a steeper stretch to the pub two thirds of the way round at Walford.

Route

Cars may be parked on the roadside near the small Hom Green Church (GR 579221) which is still within the parish of Ross. This church, built in 1903, has recently been restored. Facing the church turn left along the road towards Ross, and just beyond Hom House turn right up a pretty lane with an interesting selection of cottages. At the junction bear left and enjoy the views of the hills. Take the footpath on the right to Ball's Farm. Continue ahead through fields, gates and stiles to the railway embankment, all that now remains of the scenic Ross to Monmouth Railway, unfortunately closed in 1964. The path leads over the disused track into a meadow, and ahead there is a stile almost hidden by undergrowth. Further stiles and gates lead through the next fields before keeping to the right of Bollin Farm to join the Ross to Coleford road.

Cross the road, turn right and walk on the pavement to the next junction, where the Howle Hill turn is taken through the hamlet of Coughton. Continue ahead, signed Pontshill, passing Coughton Farm and the converted mill. The distinctive waymarks of the Wye Valley Walk lead from here to Walford. On the right the path leads uphill through fields, over stiles and along lanes to a stone dwelling on Howle Hill. Turn right along a pleasant track overlooking Chase Hill; it bears right passing an assortment of buildings before reaching the road beside Hill House.

Cross the stile opposite where the path descends to a delightful valley. A brook is crossed before a step ascent leads to cottages at Spring Hom on Bulls Hill. Cross the road where a public footpath to Walford is followed. In early spring the banks of the path are covered in snowdrops, and in autumn the dried leaves rustle under foot. At Bramble Bank Cottage on Leys Hill the waymarked path continues along a track where a great variety of wild flowers grow, above the village of Walford with its church, inn and school. As the path descends to the road opposite the sawmill, turn right leaving the Wye Valley Walk and walk through the village to the Mill Race.

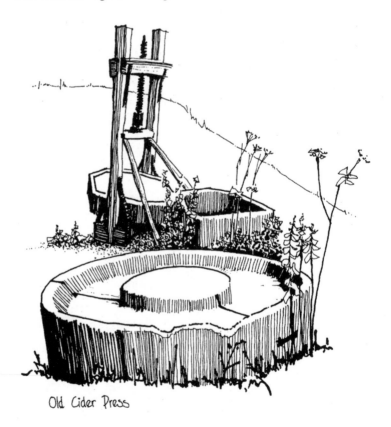

Old Cider Press

The Mill Race   (Tel: 01989 562891)

A much altered and modernised old pub, with most of the character dispensed with, the Mill Race is now a 'Gastro Pub'. It is neat and spacious and relaxed. The furnishings are modern and uniform, the floors tiled, the 'live' fire a wood burning stove. The décor is fresh and simple, with a few prints on the walls. The Award Winning chef is visible in the kitchen creating 'freshly cooked traditional English fare with Mediterranean influences'. Diners varied in age from happy, free range toddlers, to doting grandparents, and all ages in between, on the day we called

The food is sourced locally, where possible from farmers and growers using 'ethical farming techniques'. Snacks are good and tasty with brothy Homemade Soup of the Day, generously filled, freshly prepared, Sandwiches, and Baked Potatoes with various fillings. Starters from the main menu include attractive Smoked Fish Salad and good Chicken Caesar. Main Courses lean towards local, low mileage, ingredients with Warm Ragstone Goat's Cheese, Home Farm Pheasant, Maple Cured Pork Loin with Colcannon and Cider Sauce, a range of Herefordshire Steaks, with 'Real Chips'. Vegetarian options include Roast Buttered Squash with Toasted Almonds. Children, see above, are welcome, as are those with special dietary requirements.

The beer is also local and seems to come from one source at the moment, the popular and expanding, Wye Valley Brewery. It is backed up by usual favourites like Guinness and best selling lagers. The cider is supplied by the reliable, and authentic, Weston's of Much Marcle. The Wine List offers reasonably priced bottles from Chile, South Africa and New Zealand, as well as more pricey items from the more famous European regions. The low mileage alternative is from the Monnow Valley in Wales, fresh light and fragrant stuff made from lesser known grapes.

Return

From the pub turn left and proceed through the village of Walford and before the road veers to the left cross a stile. Here a signed footpath leads across the field and a brook by a wooden bridge to the thirteenth century church of St. Michael. Keep to the left of this solid building surrounded by yew trees. Iron swing gates lead out of the churchyard, and a narrow overgrown path, beside the disused railway track, leads onto Hom Green Road, which is followed to the left.

Warryfield Cottage and Farm are passed before turning right to follow a tarmac lane to Old Hill Court. Beyond this black and white house turn left along the drive also serving as a right of way to Hom Green. On meeting the lower road turn right, passing the elegant Hill Court, built in the late seventeenth century. Within a few hundred yards you are back at Hom Green Church.

Walk 9 GOODRICH CHURCH

**6 mile walk from Welsh Bicknor
to Ye Hostelrie, Goodrich
OS Explorer OL14**

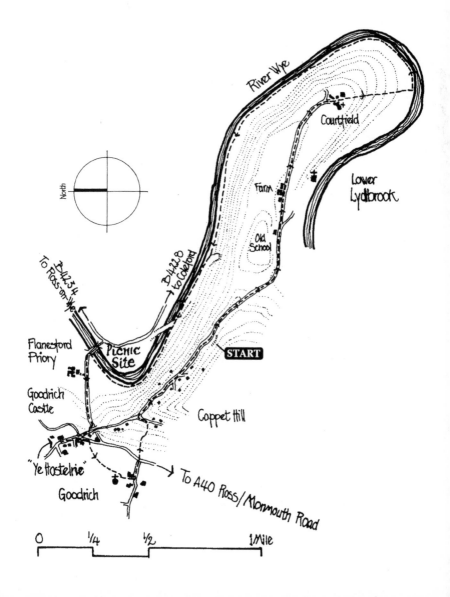

High above the Wye stands the compact village of Goodrich with it historic castle, church and priory. This easy ramble leads through the remote riverside parish of Welsh Bicknor, where an interesting route through the Courtfield estate joins the Wye Valley Walk. At Goodrich there is ample time to visit the mock Gothic inn, the ruins of the Norman castle and the thirteenth century church of St. Giles.

Route

Cars may be parked near a small disused quarry (GR583184) signed Coppet Hill Local Nature Reserve on the right hand side of the road from Goodrich to Welsh Bicknor. Walk along the road for nearly a quarter of a mile, and after passing Primrose Cottage, once the school, fork left along the private road, also a public footpath. Cottages and farm buildings are reached before the footpath continues ahead with the former monastic buildings of Courtfield on the right. The path becomes stony as it descends to a field gate, and follows along the left hand side of the field to join the Wye Valley Walk at the riverside.

Opposite are the wooded hills of the Forest of Dean above the once industrial village of Lower Lydbrook. Turn left along the waymarked walk, a pleasant route through meadows, mixed woodland and fields leading to the handsome Kerne Bridge. Along the latter section the ruins of Goodrich Castle and the barns of Flanesford Priory are in sight. In mid river you will notice several small islands, always a popular nesting site for swans.

At Kerne Bridge leave the Wye Valley Walk and turn left along the road to Goodrich. Keep to the pavement passing the entrance to the renovated Flanesford where all that remains of the original Augustinian Priory, founded in the fourteenth century, are the refectory, barns and fish ponds. Before the Dry

Flanesford Priory, Kerne Bridge & Goodrich Castle

Bridge, an unusual stone arch spanning the road, bear left up the path and steps, and turn right to cross the bridge. Follow the road down to the shop, castle entrance and inn at Goodrich.

Ye Hostelrie   (Tel: 01600 890241)

Ye Hostelrie with its strange grey stone pinnacles and turrets is at first glance like something out of a Hitchcock movie. Once inside it assumes normality and with gas fired 'logs' in one bar, and a side room, ramblers may rest awhile, enjoy a drink and a snack while watching the ever present Sky TV. The bars are beamed and floors are tiled or carpeted. A variety of prints hang on the walls including the amusing 'The Fox o' One Hill' by J.C. Dollman R. A. (1851-1934), who in his early work is said to have influenced Vincent Van Gogh.

Snacks include Baked Stuffed Field Mushrooms, Lasagna with Garlic Bread and Salad, plus a host of Baguettes with various fillings. Main courses include Steak and Wye Pie, Chicken Zorba

"Ye Hostelrie", Goodrich.

with Feta Cheese and Rice, Pork Loin with Cider Sauce, Beef Olives, and Steaks. Vegetarian Dishes and Children's Portions are also available.

A small selection of wines are available by the glass or bottle. There are various lagers and beers, including the locally brewed Butty Bach, as well as Herefordshire Cider. Quiet at lunchtimes, but locals say it positively rocks in the evenings.

Return

After rest and refreshments, retrace your way back to the castle entrance, where a signed lane leads to the historic remains of Goodrich Castle. Now in the care of English Heritage, it is open at all reasonable times, and is well worth the detour. Return to the shop and pass the Primary School, where a signed footpath on the right leads around the school to the recently formed Greenspace . Bear left here and follow this path over a shallow brook, through fields and a swing gate before reaching the churchyard.

Dedicated to St. Giles, the church has a slender fourteenth century spire, and if the key can be obtained there are items of interest to inspect, including a communion cup given to the church by Dean Swift, the Irish author of Gulliver's Travels, in memory of his grandfather, vicar of this parish during the Civil War.

Leave the church by the path on the south west side, leading between fields and high stone walls of the Old Vicarage. At the road turn left to the junction, cross the Goodrich Road to reach the stile opposite signed 'Coppet Hill and YHA'. Keep ahead up the steep field and head for the stile in the corner. This leads onto a narrow sunken path with a flight of stone steps. At the tarmac lane, the top of the northern end of Coppet Hill, there are delightful views of the Wye Valley. .

Turn left along the lane which shortly joins the Welsh Bicknor Road that is followed to the right, passing several houses and cottages built into the hillside. In the adjacent woodland, winter ramblers will notice squirrels' drays and pigeons' nests in leafless trees. Beside the road is a disused Victorian well inscribed 'Waste Not Want Not'. Continue for another few hundred yards to return to the disused quarry.

Walk 10 **LOWER LYDBROOK**

7 mile walk from English Bicknor to the Anchor Inn
OS Explorer OL14

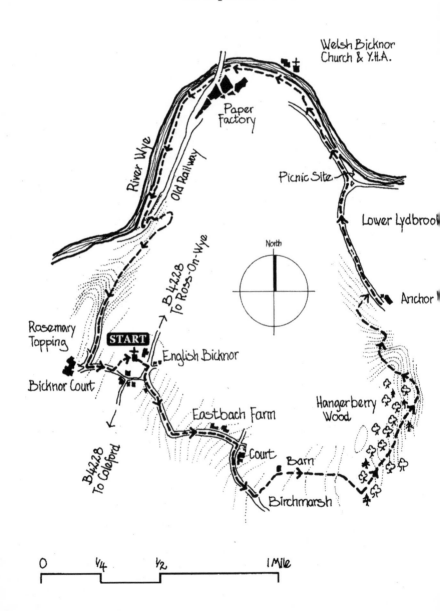

Welsh Bicknor
Church & Y.H.A.

Paper
Factory

River Wye

Old Railway

Picnic Site

Lower Lydbrook

North

B 4228
To Ross-On-Wye

Anchor

Rosemary
Topping

START

English Bicknor

Bicknor Court

B 4228
To Coleford

Eastbach Farm

Hangerberry
Wood

Court

Barn

Birchmarsh

0   ¼   ½   1 Mile

The village of English Bicknor lies mid-way between the River Wye and the Forest of Dean. The twelfth century church of St. Mary stands within the ramparts of an early Norman Castle where the wooded mound of the motte can still be seen. This walk is strenuous in places but easy to follow as most of the route is way marked along forest trails and the Wye Valley Walk. It starts from English Bicknor where a twisting metalled lane leads through remote countryside to join a forest trail which meanders down to Lower Lydbrook and the Anchor Inn.

Route

At English Bicknor there is parking behind the church (GR 581158) where a signed footpath leads through the school yard to the church and the main Ross to Coleford road. Turn right along the road and after a few yards turn left along a quiet lane to Eastbach with its rendered farmhouse and attractive Court surrounded by a high stone wall. Take the right hand fork leading around this building and follow the lane until reaching Birchmarsh Cottages, where a field path on the left, beyond the cottages, is followed towards a converted barn. Keep to the right of the barn, and cross the field gate on the right where the way ahead closely follows the right hand hedge ascending to over 600 feet before reaching a solid stile. Here catch your breath and enjoy the exhilarating views of the windswept landscape. Continue ahead to a gate leading into the forest, and turn left along the sparsely way marked forest trail. For the less robust, an alternative route from Birchmarsh Cottages is to follow the lane past a large old milestone to beyond the next cottage where a signed footpath on the left shortly joins the waymarked trail.

The yellow arrowed path leads through Hangerberry Wood with its beech, oak and larch trees, and bears left at a clearing overlooking

Lydbrook. Scars left from the iron, tin and coal mining of previous industrial days are barely visible today. It is difficult to imagine that this valley was criss-crossed with tramways, railways and viaducts to transport these products. The waymarked trail continues along a narrow rocky path descending steeply to a lane followed to the left, passing several cottages before twisting and turning through a stand of delightful beech trees. Be careful to follow the waymarked footpath leading out of the woods and across fields and stiles, and bears right to meet the road at Lower Lydbrook where a right turn along the road will lead directly to the Anchor Inn about 300 yards away. It stands opposite an attractive cottage connected with the famous eighteenth century actress, Sarah Siddons.

The Anchor Inn   (Tel: 01594 860822)
The Anchor, dating it is alleged from the 1450s, is a find in an area not brimming with good pubs. Sympathetically restored by a caring landlord it fulfills all the necessary requirements. The food is tasty and much of it is home made. A wood burning stove and several wall heaters keep the temperature in winter at a reasonable level.

Apart from the exposed beams, carpeted floors and the usual pub furniture, there is also a collection of animal traps and brass plate. Friend's paintings, and black and white pictures, many of local interest, cover the whitewashed walls.

Alan, an experienced chef, and one of the longest serving mine hosts in the Forest of Dean, offers interesting and well priced fare. His Soup - good rich cockle warming stuff, is Home Made, as is the excellent Game and Brandy pate. There are also Filled Jacket Potatoes and Sandwiches. The Mains include, Fish, Curry and Rice, and a host of tasty Pies in rich gravy, Cottage, Pheasant, Pigeon, Rabbit. The Vegetarian options are Root Pie

English   The Bicknor Churches   Welsh

and Ratatouille. All dishes are served piping hot with a choice
of potatoes and seasonable vegetables. The quality of the coffee
is above most pub standards.

The ale is from two good breweries, Cornish Jack from Sharp's, the Brewery of the Year for 2008, and Dorothy Goodbody from the Wye Valley Brewery. Murphy's Stout, Guinness and Boddington are also offered. The Cider is Stowford Press from Weston's. Wine is available by bottle and glass. There is a neat and attractive dining room for the festive or Sunday diner. Children and animals, (under control), are actively encouraged. Parking is adequate.

Return

Retrace your steps back to the last stile but continue along the road to a pleasant picnic site beside the River Wye. Turn left, following the B4228 Coleford Road, until shortly reaching a stile, the start of a signed riverside path leading through fields and bracken clad banks, where the river provides an ideal habitat for swans and wild ducks. On the opposite side of the Wye stands the church of Welsh Bicknor rebuilt just over a century ago in the Norman style, next to a rambling old vicarage, now a Youth Hostel.

The path comes close to a former paperworks, and after crossing a brook, leads to a large disused railway bridge, where the Wye Valley Walk is joined. On this walk it is only followed for a short stretch under the bridge then along the banks of the Wye with the wooded conical shape hill of Rosemary Topping ahead. A stile and a flight of steps lead onto the remains of the Ross to Monmouth railway track. Leave the Wye Valley Walk here by turning sharp left along the track to follow a waymarked path to Common Grove.

A steep climb across hilly fields and over a well-defined section of Offa's Dyke is followed with the aid of yellow arrows, these lead through more fields above great Collins Grove to arrive at a tarmac lane beside Grove Cottage. Follow this quiet lane where a gradual uphill haul, keeping left at the junction, leads to a row of cottages. Beyond these dwellings turn left through a swing gate to the car park and English Bicknor Church.

Walk 11 SEVEN SISTERS

7½ mile walk from Symonds Yat Rock
to the Saracen's Head
OS Explorer OL14

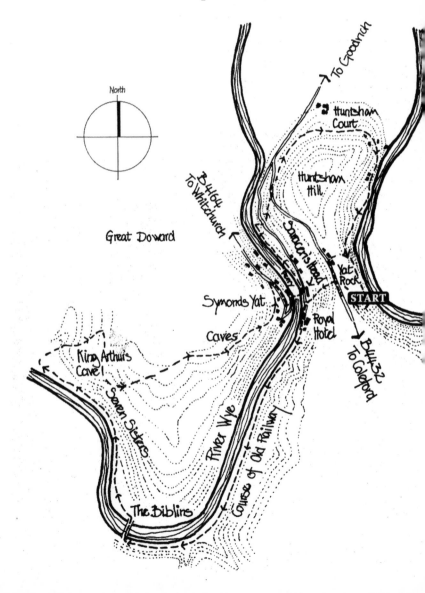

Symonds Yat is the most popular place for sightseers and walkers in the Wye Valley. The scattered village lies along the east and west banks of the River Wye where cottages, inns and hotels are attractively built in the steeply wooded slopes of this scenic gorge. There is parking on the east side at the Yat Rock car park, the start of this strenuous but interesting walk. The route, offering splendid and varied views, follows waymarked paths and the Wye Valley Walk, descending to cross the river and climb steeply to King Arthur's Cave and the Seven Sisters before re-crossing the Wye to reach the Saracen's Head. A shorter return around Huntsham Hill leads back to the Yat Rock. The ferry operates most of the year except during mid winter and adverse weather conditions. If in doubt ring 01600 890435. Change will be required for parking and the ferry.

Route

From the Symonds Yat Rock car park (GR 565159) the yellow arrows of a waymarked path are easily located leading from the log cabin. The path descends the 400 feet down to the riverside, zig-zagging through trees and down slippery steps. At the river bank by the Royal Hotel turn left where the Wye Valley Walk follows the route of the dismantled remains of the Ross to Monmouth Railway, surely one of the prettiest lines in the country when it operated between 1873 and 1964. The rapids are soon reached - a favourite stretch of water for canoeists to practise their skills. On the opposite side of the bank is the site of the New Weir iron works, a forge which existed for many centuries and was in use up to the early nineteenth century.

A mile further downstream the steeply wooded and rocky gorge widens at the Biblins, where a suspension bridge takes the walker across the river. The Wye Valley Walk continues to the left along the riverside below the tall rocky outcrops known as the Seven Sisters and disused quarries. Take care not to miss a turning on the right which follows another forest path, clearly waymarked with yellow arrows. It follows a steep, rocky path, winding above quarries and boulders before reaching King Arthur's Cave, where traces of prehistoric man and animals were discovered in 1870.

Having explored the cave, follow the waymarks through the trees to a magnificent viewpoint at the top of the Seven Sisters. From here continue to the sandstone quarry, where the forest trail veers right across a mixed woodland with, in season, several spices of fungi. Cross two forest tracks and continue until another track is met. Turn left and descend to more caves at a point where the rushing of the rapids may be heard. Keep ahead along the track to a tarmac lane, then bear right towards the river and shortly take a footpath on the left which leads to the ferry crossing, operated by the Saracen's Head on the opposite bank. Hail for the ferryman who pulls the boat across by means of a cable and collects your payment for a soothing and restful crossing.

The Saracen's Head   (Tel: 01600 890435)

This busy old free house is nicely positioned beside the Wye in a busy stretch of the valley with guest houses, hotels and cottages perched on both banks of the river. Once a cider mill, the Saracen's Head, under the same management for fourteen years, is more popular than ever. There are two bars, one a basic place with a pool table and fruit machine, the other a comfortable room with scrubbed pine tables, several bar staff ready to serve, and a view of the river.

In summer customers can loll on the grass outside, watching

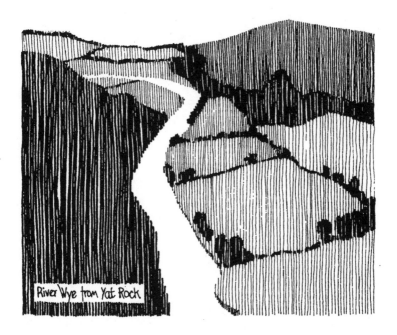

River Wye from Yat Rock

the ferryman ply his ancient trade, hauling thirsty customers over the water. Decor is simple, service is warm and efficient, and accommodation is offered. Children are welcome.

The menu is interesting with starters like, Herb Crostinis with Olives and Feta, Seared King Scallops with Sauce Capers, Black Pudding with Potatoes and Sweet Red Onion, and Linguine of Smoked Salmon with Crab and Peas and Lemon Cream. Main Courses feature, Char Grilled Steaks, Fresh Fillet of Cod in Yeast Batter, Home Made Cottage Pie with Linguine Nicoise, and Goodrich Middle White Pork Sausages with Mashed potato and Onion Gravy.

A host of Vegetarian options include; Beetroot Consommé with Sour Cream Tortellini, and Plum Tomato Tart with Olive Tapenade and Feta Dressing. Veggie Mains feature a Fricassee of Wild Mushrooms with Roasted Cocotte Potato and Silverskin Onions, and a Warm Tart of Smoked Garlic and Aubergine with

Parmesan Crackling. A good range of Local Cheese are always on offer

The Wine List contains plenty of choice, from the usual and reliable suspects like Chilean and Spanish, to more expensive bottles from France. The Beer selection offers a lip smacking range which includes, Theakston Old Peculiar, Butty Bach and HPA from the Wye Valley Brewery, a soft, hoppy offering from Butcome's, and Moreland's Speckled Hen. Enough to satisfy the most demanding Real Aler. Ciders include the excellent Weston's Stowford Press and Symond's Scrumpy Jack.

But don't over do it - the rest of this walk is strenuous.

Return

Rejoin the Wye Valley Walk beside the inn. Continue right along the riverside leaving the picturesque village to the upper ferry. Turn right, cross the road, go up the slope and follow the way marked walk across the upper road then through woods and along forest tracks. Some fine views will be enjoyed of Huntsham Court, Goodrich Church and the fern clad slopes of Coppet Hill. Notice the huge boulders of conglomerate rock, known locally as pudding stone, but do not miss a left turn down steps leading to the riverside.

A steep sunken lane leads past several ruined cottages, abandoned perhaps because of sliding boulders. The thick woods are a delight; a blend of holly, spindle, chestnut, mosses, ferns, fungi and old man's beard. At the riverside the 400 feet high Yat Rock comes into view, as one bears right away from the Wye. The ascent along the Wye Valley Walk is followed up steps, around bends, then veers left along a forest track until reaching a sign-posted junction where the Wye Valley Walk continues. Our way goes right up to Yat Rock. This narrow steep track eventually leads to several cottages, where a right turn leads to the road beside disused lime kilns.

Follow the road to the left back to the Yat Rock car park. If you still have any energy, walk over the wooden bridge you have just passed beneath, this leads to the famous view of the horseshoe bend. Then enjoy well-earned refreshments at the log cabin.

Walk 12 REDBROOK BRIDGE

6½ mile walk from the Kymin to the Boat Inn at Penalt
OS Explorer OL14

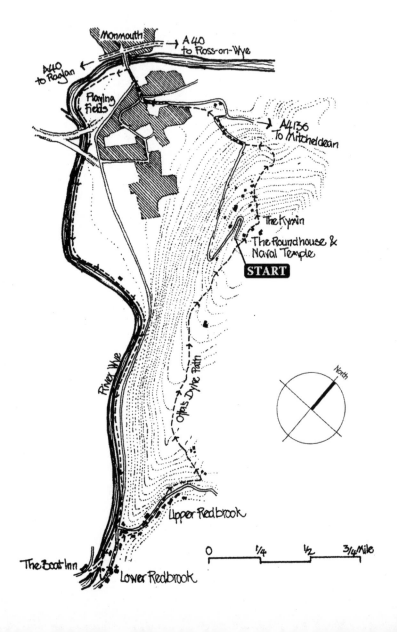

This is a splendid and scenic walk in the heart of the Wye Valley leading from the Kymin, a beauty spot standing at over 800 feet offering outstanding views over Monmouth and the Welsh hills. The route is easy to follow, along two waymarked routes, Offa's Dyke Path and the Wye Valley Walk. However, a long steep climb back to the Kymin awaits you after a welcome pause for refreshment at Redbrook Bridge. The Kymin has been managed by the National Trust since the beginning of the 20th century. The site dates back to 1793 when a group of Monmouth gentlemen created the pleasure grounds, and built the Roundhouse. In 1800 the Naval Temple was erected, commemorating sixteen famous English admirals. Two years later Lord Nelson visited the temple and said that the view was one of the finest he had ever seen.

Route

The walk begins at the National Trust car park at the Kymin (GR 528126). Follow the yellow arrows and white acorns, marking Offa's Dyke Path, which leads past the unusual Naval Temple, the white Roundhouse and the magnificent viewpoint. The route continues slightly to the left down a rocky path which disappears into thick woodland. On meeting a 'Private Road', turn immediately right across open land before entering further woods. A tarmac lane is soon reached, descending towards Monmouth until a waymarked path between fields and through woodland leads to the outskirts of the town.

This historic Welsh town of Monmouth grew around the Norman Castle and where the River Monnow joins the Wye. It has many attractive Georgian buildings and associations with Henry V, Nelson and Charles Rolls of Rolls Royce fame. Turn left along the road and immediately before the Wye Bridge turn sharp left to leave Offa's Dyke Path and join the Wye Valley Walk, waymarked with leaping salmons. From this point the path closely follows the banks of the River Wye for about three miles to Redbrook. Firstly it skirts the playing fields of Monmouth School before going under a disused railway bridge of the old Ross to Monmouth Railway, in operation from 1873 to 1965, then the path continues beneath the dismantled viaduct of the Wye Valley Railway which carried passengers from 1876 to 1956 along the route between Monmouth and Chepstow.

The remaining two miles to Redbrook are along a most delightful stretch of the Wye although in places the path is narrow and rocky. In June we counted sixteen different wild flowers including masses of comfrey, campions and vetches. Dragonflies too were enjoying the summer sun above the rippling currents of the river. Timeless scenes constantly appeared as multicoloured cows waded in and drank from the cool Wye, a clutch of ducklings swam around their mother, and fishermen either waist-high in water or sitting more comfortably in a dinghy were hoping to net a Wye salmon.

Before reaching Redbrook the railway bridge comes into view, and at the village the way-marked path leads onto the road. At a former pub the path goes right to rejoin the riverbank to Redbrook Bridge. Walk over this old rusty iron bridge, another reminder of the railway age, but now serving only as a footbridge. In its shadow stands the Boat Inn, where refreshments may be obtained before an energetic return.

The Boat Inn   (Tel: 01600 712615)

The Boat, listed in several well known guides, is situated on the sunny right hand bank of the River Wye and is the only Welsh pub in this book. It is a tiny and interesting old inn with beams,

The Roundhouse on The Kymin.

simple furniture, and a quarry tiled floor. A sweet smelling wood burning stove keeps the old place cosy during the damp days of winter.

CAMRA would probably approve of the emphasis on 'real' ales like the intriguingly named Pigswill and Doom Bar, also Butty Bach and Kingstone Challenger, the last from a tiny brewery not far from the pub. The list of ciders has a touch of quality about it too with Weston's, Gwatkin's and Gillow featured. The 'wine list', unusually excludes anything from the grape, preferring to concentrate on what could be termed hedgerow and back garden vintages. There are no fewer than twenty-one to choose from, including Parsnip and Cowslip. The landlord promises to try a few 'real' wines in 2008, 'like Australian'.

The blackboard lists Lasagne, Beer Stew and also 'a find' for us, Pan Haggerty. This is tasty, hot cheese and potato dish, cooked in olive oil, flavoured with garlic, and served with Garlic Bread and Salad. A great choice for the hungry rambler. The 'Lite

Bites' included Home Made Soup, lots of different Baguettes and Baked Potatoes. The tiny Boat is lively on Tuesday and Thursday with local blues band performing.

This is a unique setting with the Wye silently slipping under the rusting arches of the old bridge a few feet away and dark trees growing up to the skyline.

Return

Leave the Boat and retrace your steps back over the bridge, but turn right, then leave through the inn's car park to reach the main road in the centre of Redbrook. This village once boasted a busy industrial past of iron foundries, mills, a brewery, a railway, a tramway and barges on the Wye. Tinplate works remained until 1961, but the dirt and dust of the past has left Redbrook a quiet place with just a few interesting sites and memories. Rejoin Offa's Dyke Path by turning left, then past the church, built in 1873 by J.P. Seddon, who also designed the unique Italian church at Hoarwithy.

Shortly bear right up a wide track, leading between cottages and derelict mills to join the Newland Road at the unusual incline tram bridge. Follow the road to the right for a few hundred yards then bear left and steeply ascend the hills of the Forest of Dean. At the top a farm overlooks a lovely wooded valley, where the route veers left along an ancient shady lane. Extensive views of the Forest of Dean and the Wye Valley may be seen. At a converted barn leave the lane, turn right across the stile, where the path leads across fields and stiles, to reach the Kymin car park by a pair of iron gates.

The Authors

Heather Hurley as a local historian and leader of walks in Herefordshire and the Wye Valley has first hand knowledge of the rights of way. She is the author of several publications on walking and local history including Wyedean Walks, The Old Roads of South Herefordshire, Fownhope Parish Paths, History of the River Crossing at Wilton, Historic Harewood, The Story of Bill Mills, The Pubs of Ross and South Herefordshire, The Pubs of the Royal Forest of Dean and The Pubs of Monmouth, Chepstow and the Wye Valley.

She has also co-authored The Story of Ross and with Jon the first editions of Paths and Pubs of the Wye Valley, Rambles and Refreshments, The Wye Valley Walk and Family Walks in the Wye Valley.

Jon Hurley lectures, writes and lectures on the subject of wine. He has published a novel, and books on pubs, wine, and pugilism. He enjoys walking, golf, and foreign travel and, like Heather, he takes a keen interest in gardening and the countryside. His books include; It's Late Very Early a novel, The Wicked Wind, a collection of poems, Wine for Game and Fish, ., A Matter of Taste- a History of Wine Drinking in Britain, Tom Spring Bare-Knuckle Champion of All England, A Ross Anthology and Recollections of Ross.

Other titles from Fineleaf

The Old Roads of South Herefordshire
By Heather Hurley
ISBN 978-0-9534437-4-1

Personalities of the Forest of Dean
By Henry G Nicholls, first published 1863
ISBN 978-0-9534437-2-7

May Hill
Paintings and drawings by Valerie McLean
ISBN 978-0-9534437-8-9

Treatise on Cyder-Making
By Hugh Stafford, first published 1753
ISBN 978-0-9557577-1-6

Geology Explained in the Forest of Dean and Wye Valley
By William Dreghorn
ISBN 978-0-9534437-1-0

Geology Explained in the Severn Vale and Cotswolds
By William Dreghorn
ISBN 978-0-9534437-5-8

Geology Explained in South Wales
By T R Owen
ISBN 978-0-9534437-6-5

Geology Explained in the Lake District
By Robert Prosser
ISBN 978-0-9534437-7-2

Excursion from the Source of the Wye
By Mark Willett, first published 1810
ISBN 978-0-9534437-0-3

Further landscape and art titles in preparation

Fineleaf Editions, 2008
www.fineleaf.co.uk